POETS NEVER DIE

RYTHIAN BLACK

Author's Ink

POETS NEVER DIE

Contents

1	The Way to Achieve	1
2	The Rue Voice	2
3	A Song I May Sing	3
4	Blessed Are The Dishwashers	4
5	Asleep Forever	5
6	Unknown	6
7	Why Did Fall Fall?	9
8	Wap	10
9	I Feel So Cold...	11
10	Who Do They See? The Fool Or The Poetry?	12
11	Small Pleasures To Ease	13
12	How A Poet Faces Death	15
13	Vampire	16
14	Overtones From The Resonance	17
15	It Will Be Painted In Black	18
16	Ghosts And Regrets	20
17	Let's Write	21
18	The Sound Of The World Ending	22

19	The Paradox Of My Life	24
20	Color Of Snow	25
21	Two Skies And A Thin Line	26
22	Pursue Your Happiness	27
23	If Only I Knew	28
24	Meaningless Dribble	30
25	I Am Not Ready To Go	31
26	A Cold Wind On A Sunny Day In April	33
27	Like A Fairytale	34
28	A Man's Biggest Mistake	35
29	Be Perfect	36
30	The Noise	37
31	The Pain	38
32	The Green	39
33	Touched By The Devil	40
34	Whether By Devil Or Angel	41
35	Lies	42
36	Duty	43
37	Just Walk Away	44
38	My Black Parade	45
39	Can't Shake The Pressure, Can't Shake The Pleasure	46
40	Finding Myself In That Purple Void	47
41	Is This Jaded?	48
42	Oh, To Be Born Again	49

43	Humanity	50
44	Punishers	51
45	Curse Me, Curse Me	52
46	The Sad Part Of Death	53
47	My Day	55
48	The Silver Wall	56
49	A Flower In A Field	57
50	Therapist In A Pocket	58
51	Realization	59
52	The Arsonist	60
53	What Is Affection?	61
54	Fall Is Upon Us	62
55	I Will Find You	63
56	Shores Warm	65
57	Almost Had It	66
58	Broke And Hope	67
59	Mr. Poe	68
60	What I Wish Upon A Star	69
61	A Bad Feeling	70
62	The Secunda And The Rain	71
63	Home And Alone	72
64	Alone	73
65	Black Pencil	74
66	Nine Billion Years	75

67	Is Charity Worth The Poverty	76
68	Poem, I Forgot	77
69	November	78
70	It's Snowing	79
71	Haunted	80
72	Melancholy In B7th	81
73	The Rustling Of The Wind	82
74	Fire In The Endless	83
75	He Who Made My School Days Bright	84
76	A City Of Woodlands	85
77	What I Do To The Art	86
78	Way Back When	87
79	Under A Scarlet Moon	88
80	Moronics	90
81	My People	91
82	Melancholic Misery	92
83	The Way They Talk	93
84	Where Do I Belong?	94
85	What Is The Darkness?	95
86	Deadwood	96
87	A Windy Day	97
88	It Is Raining	98
89	My Friend The Moon	99
90	At The Faire	100

91	Cry You Mortals	101
92	The Queen Of Instruments	102
93	The Beauty and Tragedy Of A Stogie	103
94	For You, For Me, For It	104
95	Snap Twice	105
96	To My Brother, To My Friend, To My Fellow Poet.	106

Copyright © 2024 by Rythian Black

All rights reserved. No part of this book may be reproduced in any manner whatsoever without written permission except in the case of brief quotations embodied in critical articles and reviews.

First Printing, 2024

I

The Way to Achieve

DREAMS ARE JUST THAT, DREAMS. IT IS UP TO YOU TO MAKE THEM INTO REALITY. TO ACHIEVE YOUR DREAMS, YOU MUST PUT WORK INTO YOUR WORK. SHARE YOUR LOVE FOR THE ART WITH PEOPLE WHO DON'T CARE.

2

The Rue Voice

I DO POETRY BECAUSE.
I CANNOT SPEAK WITH SPEECH.
ONLY WRITE WITH WORDS.
MY VOICE IS NOT VOCAL.
ONLY MY PROSE IS POTENT.
EVEN THEN.

3

A Song I May Sing

A GUITAR AND A CAPTAIN IN HAND.
PLAYING SONGS WITHOUT A BAND.
SINGING WHAT I CAN, ABOUT WHAT I CAN'T.

IN A CROWED I SEE A SEA OF FANS.
THERE FOR MY ART.

4

Blessed Are The Dishwashers

BLESSED ARE THE DISHWASHERS
WHO GROVEL IN PISS AND SHIT
BLESSED ARE THE DISHWASHERS
WHO ARE DRENCHED IN MUCK AND SPIT

5

Asleep Forever

I JUST WANT TO BE A SHELL, LIFELESS, DRIFTING THROUGH AN ENDLESS SEA OF SPACE AND VOID ADRIFT

6

Unknown

TO THOSE THEY WISH TO HIDE

TO YOU THE BEAUTIFUL PEOPLE I WILL NOT HIDE.

THE TRUTH AND REASON, PEOPLE WILL NOT ABIDE.

I DON'T SPEAK ILL OR WISH TO HURT THE INNOCENT.

UNLIKE THE BASTARDS I WILL NOT DISCRIMINATE.

I WILL BE HONEST AND TRUE ABOUT WHAT THEY THINK...

YOU ARE NOT WANTED; YOU WILL NEVER BE WANTED.

YOUR PRESENCE IN THEIR "PERFECT" LIVES MAKES THEM DAUNTED.

IT IS NOT YOURS TO BLAME THEY CANNOT ACCEPT YOU.

NO MATTER WHAT YOU DO, THEY WILL NEVER COME TO.

YOU BE YOU; NOT WHAT SOCIETY WISHES YOU WEREN'T.

BE BEAUTIFUL, BE INSPIRING, BE NOT THEM.

BECAUSE NO MATTER WHAT, THEY WILL ALWAYS BE SCUM

THEY FEAR YOU, YOUR PURE UNCORRUPTED KINDNESS.

SO MUCH SO ALL THEY SEE IS PURE, HATRED, BLINDNESS.

DO NOT HIDE, DO NOT HIDE, DO NOT HIDE, DO NOT

HIDE...

7

Why Did Fall Fall?

USUALLY, I'M HAPPY WHEN FALL ARRIVES. BUT NOW FALL SEEMS TO ME TO BE A TRADITIONAL SENSE OF GLOOMY.

8

Wap

WHEN I CAUGHT A GLIMPSE OF THE PINK BACKGROUND AND THEN THE FAINT BLURRY IMAGE BEGAN TO CLEAR IN MY EYES I FELT A SLIGHT FEAR. THEN WHEN IT BECAME FULLY CLEAR I FELT A SHIVER AND CHILL OF HORROR ON MY SPINE AND BACK. LIKE A COLD EMPTY WIND OF HOLLOW NOTHINGNESS.

THEN ANY SEMBLANCE OF HAPPINESS IN MY LIFE WAS SNUFFED OUT BY PURE CRINGINESS AND ANGER. I HAVEN'T FELT THIS MUCH HATRED IN ME SINCE I FIRST DISCOVERED THE HORRID, ABSURD, DISGRACENESS AND PURE UNDYING CRINGE OF THE DREADFUL TIKTOK... I MAY NEVER RECOVER FROM THIS COSMIC HORROR.

9

I Feel So Cold…

I HAVE ALWAYS SEEN MYSELF AS AN HONEST MAN. BUT HERE TODAY I FOUND MYSELF. I CONVINCED MYSELF. I BEGGED MYSELF. I TOLD MYSELF. THAT I COULD NEVER LIE. I GUESS YOU COULD SAY I WASN'T LYING. AS I TRULY BELIEVED MYSELF TO BE HONEST.

10

Who Do They See? The Fool Or The Poetry?

I DO NOT DO MUCH READING NOWADAYS.

I BARELY HAVE TIME BETWEEN ALL WORK AND NO PLAY.

THE KIND OF READING I DO NOW IS OF FACES.

I READ THE WAY THEY TALK, LOOK AND HEAR ME.

THEY LOOK AS IF IT IS INCONCEIVABLE OF ME WRITING POETRY.

THEY HEAR ME AS IF I'M NOT EVEN SPEAKING.

11

Small Pleasures To Ease

WORK IS DONE, IT'S TIME FOR FUN.
THE DAY WAS HARD AND NIGHT.
I RAISED MY STEAKS AND THEN WON.
I PROVED THAT I AM RIGHT.
I BOUGHT A LONG CIGAR.
I SAT OUTSIDE AND SMOKED ALL NIGHT LONG.
LISTENED TO A SINGING GUITAR.
AND MADE MY OWN THEME SONG.

I FOUND MYSELF THOUGHT IN DEEP.
THINKING THAT I SHOULD WRITE.
INSTEAD, I DECIDED TO SLEEP...
WITH A CIGAR LIT BRIGHT.

ASLEEP IN THE COLD PEACEFUL DARK.

THEN I AWAKE IN THE BRIGHT

UNREADY FOR THE DAY TO START

THEN IT'S BACK TO THE BLIGHT

12

How A Poet Faces Death

WRITERS, POETS, ARTISTS...
ALL OF US ARE THE SAME IN THE END.
WE FIGHT AND DIE DOING WHAT WE LOVE.
THIS DRIVE TO CREATE IS SO GREAT THAT WE
MAY DIE IN THE MIDST OD OUR AR-

13

Vampire

WELCOME TO MY GOTHIC CASTLE

SUNLIGHT FADES TO CANDLELIGHT

WHERE EVERYBODY IS GRACILE.

DRESS IN BLACK AND SHADOWED NIGHT.

BATS, COFFINS, SKULLS, ROSES, NO LIGHT IN SITE...

ESCAPE HUMANITY'S HASSLE

JOIN THE MURDER AND TAKE THE FLIGHT...

14

Overtones From The Resonance

A GUITAR STRING DOESN'T PLAY ON ITS OWN, EVEN WHEN SOLELY PLUCKED. PLUCK A STRING THEM STOP IT. AND LISTEN. YOU HERE OVERTONES FROM THE RESONANCE OF THE SINGLE STRING. MUSIC DESPITE A NOTE.

15

It Will Be Painted In Black

I SEE MYSELF IN A MEMORY, FROM A LIFE LONG AGO.

FUNNY HOW FIVE YEARS FEELS FOREVER.

I SEE A PODIUM, PILLARS OF CANDLES, DRAPERY OF ACCEPTABLE REDS, SICKLY BLUES AND BLINDING WHITES.

TWO SCORE OF STARING EYES, LOOKING TO ME DAWNED IN A MISERABLE TAN GARMENT, FULL OF PATRIOTIC COLORS OF A CORRUPT NATION.

AT THIS TIME, I HAD A CHANGED MINE, WISHING TO DROWN THE RAINBOW IN INK AND SHADOW. TO PAINT THE RITUAL IN BLACK.

MAKE THE DAY OF REWARD FOR MY YEARS OF SERVICE AND WORK SPECIAL AND UNIQUE.

BUT MY WISHES AND INDIVIDUALISM WERE

DENIED, AND MY SPECIAL DAY WAS PUT IN BINDER LINED IN RED, WHITE AND BLUE.

SO NOW, YEARS AFTER... EVERYTHING I DO, EVERYTHING I SEE. MY SHORT LIFE WILL BE PAINTED IN A BEAUTIFUL PURE BLACK.

16

Ghosts And Regrets

WHY DO THE DEAD LINGER?
NOT RESTING IN THE GRAVE.
DANCING WITH THE TOMBSTONES.

DID THEY NOT HEAR HELL CALL?

OR THE GRIM BELLRINGER?
WHY DO THEY DRESS LIKE SLAVES?
WEARING CHAINS OF DREAD WOES.

17

Let's Write

LET US WRITE A POEM TOGETHER. LET US SHARE EACH OTHER'S THOUGHTS, DREAMS, FANTASIES. NIGHTMARES AND ALL.

TELL ME ABOUT YOUR CHILDHOOD SO I CAN EXPERIENCE LONGING HAPPINESS IN MY ADULTHOOD.

MAKE A SONNET ABOUT WHERE YOU ARE FROM, WHERE YOU ARE BORN, YOUR HOME, SO THAT I CAN FIND MY OWN.

SHOW ME HOW IT FEELS TO BE FULFILLED WITH SATISFACTION WITH ONESELF. SO, I CAN WRITE IT, AND STUFF THE PAPER IN A BOOKSHELF.

READ ME YOUR LIFE, SO I CAN BE ENRAGED WITH JEALOUSY AND STRIFE.

SING ME A SONG, ABOUT LOVE, WITHOUT SAYING SO LONG.

18

The Sound Of The World Ending

WHAT DO YOU THINK THE WORLD ENDING WOULD SOUND LIKE? WOULD YOU HEAR... EARTH SHATTERING QUAKES AS THE GLOBE CRACKS AND SHAKES. WOULD YOU HEAR FLOOM AND GUSTING WINDS AND FRIARY DOOM? OR WOULD YOU HEAR NOTHING AS YOUR EARDRUMS POP AS THE AIR ESCAPES THE WORLD, AND YOU DROP. WOULD YOU HEAR. HORNS. AND SEE A BLINDING WHITE AS YOU ARE LEFT BEHIND IN ENDLESS NIGHT. YOU KNOW WHAT I WOULD HEAR. MUSIC... AS A COMET FALLS FROM STARS, IN PERFECT FASHION HURTLING SEEMINGLY AT THE PERFECT MOMENT IN TIME, DRIFTING IN SILENCE THROUGH NOTHING, THEN IT CATCHES AFLAME LIKE A FLINT. AS IT FALLS WILLINGLY TO DESTROY EVERYTHING, MUSIC IS ALL I HEAR. A GENTLE SOUND OF A MUSIC BOX TO MY MELANCHOLIC MELODIES. EVERYTHING ELSE IS

QUIET AROUND ME AS I ALONE SIT AND WATCH THE SKY TURN A BEAUTIFUL FALL ORANGE. EVERYTHING ELSE IS RUNNING, THE BIRDS TRY AND FLY AWAY ONLY TO BE MET WITH BLAZING WIND AND WINGS. THE DEER ARE FROZEN STIFF FROM SHOCK. THE PEOPLE TERRIFIED WITH FEAR AND UTTER AWE, RUN OR HIDE TO NO AVAIL. ME I JUST SIT THERE AND LISTEN TO THE SOFT PIANO, OR THE GENTLE GUITAR, THE WORLD IS GETTING BRIGHTER, MY CHAIR RATTLES IN THE DIRT, AND MY DRINK SPILLS. AND MY CIGAR IGNITES WITHOUT A MATCH. THE SCREAMS ARE DEAFENING TO ME, ONLY THE SOFT GENTLE MUSIC IS ALL I CARE TO HEAR AS TAKE A PUFF...

19

The Paradox Of My Life

I WANT TO BE HAPPY, BUT WHEN I'M HAPPY I SAY SOMETHING STUPID OR SILLY.

AFTERWARDS I BECOME SAD OR ANGRY, THEN I STAY QUIET AND BITE MY TONGUE, SOMETIMES LITERALLY. I AM THINKING ABOUT GETTING RID OF IT ENTIRELY.

20

Color Of Snow

COUNTLESS, IS ALL I CAN SAY. COLORS HIDDEN IN THE GRAINS OF SNOW LAID UPON THE GROUND FOR DAYS. VIOLETS OVERLAPPING HAYS OF SCARLET GREENS AND HUES OF AUTUMN SILVER GRAYS. EVEN BRIGHTER SHADES OF WHITE THAN THE BLINDING SNOW IN MY EYES. LIKE STARLIGHT IN THE SKY. I'VE ONLY EVER SEEN SUCH BEAUTY IN THE DEAD EXPANSE OF ENDLESS NIGHT. NEVER ONCE IN THE BRIGHTEST OF ALL MY OLD YOUNG DAYS.

21

Two Skies And A Thin Line

TAKING A JOURNEY FAR FROM HOME. I WAS CAPTURED BY THE SEA, AWESTRUCK AND QUITE STUCK GAZING AT WHAT I COULD ONLY DESCRIBE AS TWO SKIES MEETING AT A THIN BLOOD RED LINE. THE SUN WAS GUILLOTINED AND BLEEDING ON THE HORIZON BETWEEN TWO SKYLINES.

22

Pursue Your Happiness

ONCE ON THE ROAD HOME, DURING THE TIME OF FALLEN LEAVES AND DEAD TREES, AFTER MY FIRST GREAT ADVENTURE. I WAS GREETED BY A MESSAGE, A SIGN. IN LITERAL MEANING. IT SPOKE TO ME AND TOLD ME TO "PURSUE YOUR HAPPINESS". THAT IS WHEN I DECIDED TO WORK TOWARDS WHAT I AM PASSIONATE.

23

If Only I Knew

IF ONLY I KNEW... HOW TO MAKE MY DREAMS, BECOME TRUE...

IF ONLY YOU KNEW... IN MY YOUTH...

IF ONLY YOU KNEW... WHAT I WAS GOING THROUGH...

I'M JUST OVER TWENTY-TWO... NOT EVEN PAST MY DUE...

BUT EVEN NOW... I CAN FEEL THE NOOSE...

CAN YOU PLEASE TELL ME... WHAT I HAVE TO DO...?

TO CHANGE MY LIFE, TO START ANEW...

IF ONLY I KNEW... HOW TO START ANEW...

IF ONLY I KNEW... HOW TO MAKE DREAMS COME TRUE...

I WANT TO RIP OFF MY MASK, TO HIDE WHAT

HAST, I WANT TO RID MYSELF OF THE OUTCAST, I WANT TO BE SOMETHING BEAUTIFUL AT LAST. OUTLAST THE CREATURE I WAS YEARS PAST...

I WANT TO BREAK THROUGH... I WANT TO START ANEW...

THE CREATURE THEY KNEW... I WANT TO BE SLEW...

I WANT TO WALK DOWN, THE GOTHIC AVENUE...

I WANT TO SHED THIS LIGHT, THAT BLINDS ME IN MY EYES, I DON'T WANT TO HIDE WHAT'S INSIDE AND TAKE FLIGHT IN THE NIGHT!

I WANT TO LET OUT THE DARK, THE SHADOWS THAT ARE SO STARK... SHOW THE WORLD WHAT'S IN MY HEART.

24

Meaningless Dribble

IN WRITTEN FORM, I LIKE TO THINK I COME OFF POETIC AND PROFOUND. IN SPOKEN WORD, I KNOW I COME OFF AS IDIOTIC WITH MEANINGLESS DRIBBLE. IT IS QUITE MISERABLE.

25

I Am Not Ready To Go

I AM NOT AFRAID OF DEATH,
OR WHAT IS, THE LACK OF LIFE.
BUT RIGHT NOW, MY KNIFE
IS ON HOLD TO TAKE MY BREATH.
I WILL NOT MEET THE REAPER.
THE BONE MAN WHO HOLDS THE SCYTHE.
THERE IS STILL SO MUCH TO DO.
SO MUCH WORK NEEDED TO BE DONE,
BEFORE I ENTER HELL'S QUEUE.
MY BOOK NEEDS TO WEIGH A TON,
I NEED A GOTHIC CASTLE,
MY BODY NEEDS TO BE THIN,
BEFORE THEY DECIDE THE TIME.

I MUST FIND THE LOVE WITHIN,
I STILL HAVEN'T REACHED MY PRIME.
I AM NOT READY TO DIE.
I HAVE ALL ETERNITY,
OR PERHAPS JUST TOMORROW.
UNTIL I GO CHEERFULLY.
AFTER MY LIFE'S LONG SORROW.
GIVE THE ABSENCE AN EMBRACE.
PERHAPS AFTER I AM GONE,
SOMEONE WILL FINALLY CARE.
ONE MIGHT EVEN CARE TO YAWN,
PERHAPS ONE MIGHT SHED A TEAR.
WHEN THEY READ SECUNDA.

26

A Cold Wind On A Sunny Day In April

STALKS AND BUDS DARE TO BUD AND STALK UP.
DON'T THEY KNOW THE WIND IS COLD?
DO THEY CARE THEY ARE GOING TO DIE?
WHEN THE SNOW FALLS FROM THE SKY.

27

Like A Fairytale

I LONG TO GIVE A GIRL A WOMAN A BEAUTIFUL, WONDERFUL LIFE, TAKE THEM AWAY FROM THEIR MUNDANE AND SHOW THEM THE BEAUTIFUL MACABRE. TAKE THEM A RIDE DOWN THE GOTHIC AVENUE OF DARKNESS AND UNKNOWN HIDDEN LOVE. MAKE THEM A GOTHIC CASTLE HIGHER THAN THE CHURCHES, WALK DOWN MYSTERIOUS DEAD WOODS. LIKE A GRIMM FABLE AND FAIRYTALE BUT THOSE ARE NEVER GRANTED, NEVER ACHIEVED. MAYBE FOR THE LENGTH OF A DREAM.

28

A Man's Biggest Mistake

THE BIGGEST MISTAKE FOR A GUY.
IS TO ASK A WOMAN WHY.

29

Be Perfect

BE PERFECT. BE PERFECT. BE PERFECT... NEVER RAISE YOUR VOICE AGAINST AUTHORITY, YET DO NOT WEEP. SAVE YOURSELF TROUBLE BY NOT SAVING OTHERS. NEVER TAKE TO DRINK BUT TAKE AS MANY PAIN KILLERS AS YOU CAN. ALWAYS BE QUICK TO JUDGE, BE QUICK TO SET THE GALLOWS. THE PYRE, THE FIRE. THE BRANDING IRON, BE THE PERFECT PUPPET. WITHOUT A SOUL, WITHOUT A HEART. NEVER MAKE A MISTAKE IT WILL COME BACK TO HAUNT YOU WHEN YOU LEAST EXPECT IT. AND YOU WILL BE HAUNTED BY YOUR PAST UNTIL YOU PERISH, SO BE PERFECT.

30

The Noise

THE NOISE, THE NOISE, I WANT TO DROWN OUT THE NOISE. THE SOUND ALL AROUND.

THE NOISE THE NOISE, THE CAT SCRATCHING AT THE DOOR, THE WHORE THROWING UP ON THE FLOOR.

THE UNEVEN BUMPS IN THE NIGHT, THE NIGHTMARE TERRORS OF FRIGHT.

THE HORRORS THROUGHOUT THE DAY. ALCOHOL IS THE WAY, TO FIND THE SILENT GAY.

31

The Pain

I DON'T FEEL A THING, I AM DULL TO THE BRAIN. ALL MY SENSES ARE NOT MY OWN, I CAN'T FEEL A THING. I CAN'T EVEN SEE WHAT'S IN FRONT OF ME, ONLY BEHIND. ALL I CAN SEE IS THE PAIN. THE GENTLE PAIN. THE SWEET MISERABLE PAIN. NOTHING ELSE HURTS BUT THE PAIN OF LOVING NO ONE.

32

The Green

THE ONLY THING I NEED TO ACHIEVE MY DREAM
IS THE SACRED GREEN.

33

Touched By The Devil

AND WHEN I WAS LEFT IN THE DARK FOR SO MANY YEARS, I LOOKED UP AND SAW HIM. STANDING AT A FORKED ROAD, WEARING A CROWN OF THORNS. NEXT TO HIM WAS ANOTHER WEARING A GOLDEN CROWN OF THORNS.

34

Whether By Devil Or Angel

IF I EVER PRAYED, IF I EVER BEGGED. IF I EVER ASKED FOR ANYTHING, PLEADED FOR SOMETHING PERSONAL. I WOULD ASK A DEVIL OR AN ANGEL. GRANT ME THE IMMORTALITY I SEEK. LIFT, AID OR HOLD ME UP HIGH ABOVE. WHETHER FROM AN ASHEN CLOUD OR IN A WHIMSICAL FOG. ANGEL, CURSE ME FOR MY SELFISH DESIRE, DEVIL BLESS ME FOR THE SIMPLEST OF WISHES. I DO NOT NEED TO STAND BESIDE EITHER OF YOU DEITIES, DEMONIC OR SLIGHTLY LESS. I JUST WISH TO STAND TALLER THAN I EVER HAVE. EVEN ON MY MOUNTAINOUS HILLS I CALL HOME. LET ME BE KNOWN IN MY LITTLE WORLD AS A LORD. ALONE, APART FROM THE COMMON RABBLE OF MY LAND OF WOES, MISFORTUNES AND MY LOATHSOME, LONESOME ROADS.

35

Lies

WE HAVE BEEN LIED TO OUR WHOLE LIVES. IN OUR SCHOOLS. COLUMBUS NEVER DISCOVERED AMERICA AND DREAMS NEVER COME TRUE. WE WERE BROUGHT UP BELIEVING THE WORLD WAS OURS TO MAKE OF. NO. I, WE WERE BORN AND BRED TO FEED THE WOLVES OF INDUSTRY AND CORPORATION. REMEMBER TO RAISE YOUR HAND. SIT WITH EYES FRONT. YES SIR...

36

Duty

AS A WRITER, WE HAVE A RESPONSIBILITY, A DUTY. WHETHER THROUGH POETRY OR ANOTHER MEANS OF WRITING. OUR OBLIGATION, OUR OBJECTIVE. IS TO WRITE, CREATE, BRING LIFE TO OUR PITIFUL AND RATHER MUNDANE LIVES. DISCOVER IMAGINATION AND MAKE OUR STORIES, MORE MAGICAL.

37

Just Walk Away

JUST WALK AWAY, LEAVE THEM ALONE, BY THEMSELVES. LEAVE THEM. LET THEM BE, THEY WILL SURVIVE, THOUGH SEVERELY WOUNDED. THEY WILL ENDURE, THOUGH FOR SURE. THEY WILL BE HURT. THIS TIME, THINK FOR YOURSELF. PURSUE YOUR HAPPINESS. WHY SUFFER, SQUABBLE AND LIVE IN PAIN FOR OTHERS. WHEN YOU CAN DREAM, LIVE IN LOVE AND JOY. ALL YOU NEED TO DO IS WALK AWAY.

38

My Black Parade

SKELETONS SMOKING STOGIES.
WEREWOLVES WHISTLING WASHINTS.
RAVENS RAVING RAVENOUSLY.
VAMPIRES VIBING VIGOROUSLY.
DEMONS DANCING DELICIOUSLY.
ACROSS A FIELD OF GREEN.
PHANTASMAL PHENOMENAL PHANTOMS.
ZEALOUS ZESTFUL ZEITGEISTS.
GHOSTLY GORGEOUS GOTHS.
HORNS HARROWING HOWLS.
BAROQUE BANJOS BLASTING.
THROUGH A DECREPIT CITY.

39

Can't Shake The Pressure, Can't Shake The Pleasure

TAKE A SWIG OF POISON, TAKE A BREATH OF EMBERS.

EASE THE STRESS OF ANNOYANCE, FOR EVERY INCONVENIENCE.

40

Finding Myself In That Purple Void

I FIND MYSELF DRIFTING, SWIMMING. FLOATING AMIDST AN IMMORTAL VOID OF BLACK, I FIND MYSELF HERE OFTEN, WHEN I'M ALONE WITH MY THOUGHTS AND THE GIFT OF SOLITUDE.

41

Is This Jaded?

I USED TO LAUGH, SMILE, BE KIND AND
CHEERFUL. I STILL DO THOUGH I AM NO
LONGER HAPPY WHEN I COMMIT. IS THIS WHAT
IT MEANS TO BE JADED.

42

Oh, To Be Born Again

OH, TO BE BORN AGAIN, BLESSED WITH CURSED KNOWLEDGE OF WHO YOU ARE AND WHAT YOU DID. WOULD YOU BE ANY DIFFERENT? OR MAKE THE SAME MISTAKES? CHANGE YOUR NAME? PERHAPS. PROBABLY NOT.

43

Humanity

IF I COULD DESCRIBE HUMANITY IN ONE WORD IT WOULDN'T BE ENOUGH. EVIL IS A GOOD TERM OUR SPECIES. WHETHER IT BE MAJOR OR MINOR. THE FAULT IS NOT OF A COMMUNITY, IF WE FIND SOMEONE WHO HAS MADE A MISTAKE IN THE FAR DISTANT PAST. WE HANG THEM IN THE SQUARE. WE SHOW THOSE WOULD BE MONSTERS OUR HUMILITY. LIKE BARING OUR TEETH LIKE FANGS WITHOUT MERCY.

44

Punishers

WHAT THE WORLD NEEDS MORE THAN ANYTHING IS LESS PUNISHERS. WHAT WE NEED IS LESS JAILERS. NO EXECUTIONERS. WHAT WE NEED IS LESS TORTURERS. WHAT WE NEED IS MORE THERAPY, MORE UNDERSTANDING, MORE MORALITY. AND LESS HUMANITY.

45

Curse Me, Curse Me

CURSE MY WAY WITH WORDS.
TO HELL WITH MY TERRIBLE THOUGHTS.
DO AWAY WITH MY WHOLE BEING.
CURSE ME, CURSE ME. DEVIL CURSE ME.
DAMN MY MOUTH AND TONGUE IN NON-SYNCH.
PLAGUING ME WITH THE ILLUSION OF IMBECILITY.

46

The Sad Part Of Death

THE SADDEST PART OF DEATH IS THE FACT THAT IT IS THE ONLY TIME YOU ARE REMEMBERED. AND EVEN THEN, YOU ARE FORGOTTEN.

HERE IS MY PREDICTION FOR WHAT WOULD HAPPEN TO ME.

I WILL DIE BEFORE MY PRIME. IN A TIME OF MISERY AND PAIN MY BLOOD WILL RAIN. FROM MOST LIKELY A SHIT LUCK TRAGEDY.

AFTER I AM DEAD AND GONE, AFTER I AM A QUIET VOID. MY LAST WISHES WILL NOT BE GRANTED. MY EVEN MORE EMPTY HUSK OF A BODY WILL BE USED AND ABUSED. TREATED LIKE PROPERTY, BY SOMEBODY WHO DOESN'T OWN

ME, KNOW ME. MY BODY MY LIFE MY ENTIRE EXISTENCE, DISGRACED.

PUMPED FULL OF CHEMICALS. MAKEUP PLASTERED ON MY FACE.

CLOTHED NOT IN BLACK PURITY BUT IN RED, WHITE AND BLUE UGLY.

47

My Day

I AM BACK HOME FOR THE DAY. SITTING OUTSIDE IN THE RAIN, A CIGAR IN MY HAND, A DRINK IN THE OTHER. WRITING POEMS IN MY NAME. IT IS IN THIS KIND OF DAY I AM AT EASE WITH PAIN.

48

The Silver Wall

ALL MY LIFE I HAVE BEEN STANDING AT A SILVER WALL.

MY WHOLE LIFE I CAN SEE IN THE ALUMINUM.

I HAVE WASTED MY WHOLE LIFE FILTHY AND DISGRACED.

BLEEDING ONTO ANOTHER PERSON'S PLATE.

I FEAR MY LIFE WILL BE NOTHING BUT THIS GRAVE STATE.

I FEEL MY LIFE WILL BE THIS UNTIL I SLEEP BENEATH A GRAVE SLATE...

49

A Flower In A Field

THERE IS A BEAUTY IN THE RARITY OF A SOLITARY FLOWER IN A MEADOW.

50

Therapist In A Pocket

POETRY IS MORE THAN JUST PRETTY WORDS TO ME.

IT IS ONE OF MY CLOSEST FRIENDS.

IT LISTENS TO ME.

GIVES ME PEACE OF MIND.

51

Realization

I'VE REALIZED NOW MUCH TOO LATE IN MY LIFE THAT PEOPLE DO NOT WANT TO BE HAPPY. THEY LOVE THE MISERY. THEY CRAVE TO BE PITIED.

52

The Arsonist

WHEN YOU ARE HATED YOU ARE HATED YOUR WHOLE LIFE. YOU CRAVE ANY AMOUNT OF AFFECTION YOU CAN GAIN. LIKE AN ARSONIST TO THE FLAME.

53

What Is Affection?

WHAT IS AFFECTION?

IS IT A SIMPLE HUG FROM A STRANGER OR A LOVER?

IS AFFECTION THE PLUCK OF A HEART? OR JUST A PUNCH TO THE HEAD?

IS AFFECTION LOVE OR LUST?

I KNOW HOW IT FEELS TO GIVE AFFECTION.

BUT I DO NOT KNOW HOW IT FEELS TO RECEIVE AFFECTION.

54

Fall Is Upon Us

FALL IS COMING.
I CAN SEE IT IN THE TREES.
I CAN SMELL IT ON THE BREEZE.
I HAVE BEEN WORKING HERE FOR A YEAR.
ALL I CAN SAY, IS I HOPE I HAVE A WONDERFUL DAY.

55

I Will Find You

I AM LOST, IN A SHADOW.
I AM GONE, IN THE SMOKE.
I AM ALONE, IN THE DARK.

ONE DAY, THERE WILL BE A BLACK RAINBOW.
ONE DAY, I WILL LOVE TO JOKE.
ONE DAY, I WILL WRITE FROM THE HEART.

MY FRIEND, MY DEAREST FRIEND.
MY LOVE, MY ONE SWEET LOVE.
MY MUSE, MY INSPIRING MUSE.

THOUGH OUR DREAMS ARE FAR, THEY WILL COME TRUE.

WHEN WE ARE TOGETHER, NOT FOR A DAY OR TIME.

I WILL FIND MY JOY, WHEN I FIND YOU.

56

Shores Warm

SHORES WARM ARE OFTEN AFTER A STORM.

57

Almost Had It

LOVE ALMOST FOUND ME.

BARELY HEALING MY MELANCHOLY, JUST BARELY.

IT WAS ALMOST, ALMOST SOMETHING.

58

Broke And Hope

SHOULD I STAY UNHAPPY AND WEALTHY?
OR GO FOR BROKE AND HOPE?
EITHER TODAY OR MAYBE SOMEDAY.
NO MATTER WHAT I FLY OR DIE.
MOST LIKELY THE LATTER THAN THE FORMER.
SHOULD I LIVE IN SORROW SHAME?
OR CHASE THAT NON-EXISTENT FAME?

59

Mr. Poe

DID YOU EVER THINK MR. POE
THAT YOU WOULD BE REMEMBERED AS SO?
DID YOU EVEN KNOW MR. POE
THAT YOU WOULD BE SO WELL KNOWN?
DO YOU EVER THINK MR. POE
THAT MAYBE I CAN BE AS SO? NO...

60

What I Wish Upon A Star

I WISH I COULD SPEAK CLEARLY AND FLUENTLY.
SO THAT I CAN BE TAKEN SERIOUSLY.

61

A Bad Feeling

EVERY NIGHT I SIT AND STARE AT MY KNIFE, THINKING. JUST THINKING.

I AM A FOOL, BUT NOT THAT MUCH A FOOL.

62

The Secunda And The Rain

THE RAIN, THE RAIN OH HOW I LOVE THE RAIN.

THE NIGHT, THE NIGHT OH HOW I LOVE THE NIGHT.

THE SENYA, THE SENYA OH HOW I LOVE THE SENYA.

63

Home And Alone

I AM AGAIN HOME, SAD AND ALONE TONIGHT.

A USUAL VISUAL TO MY AND MANY EYES.

ME ALONE WITHOUT EVEN THE LUXURY OF A WOMAN'S COMPANY. NOTHING LIKE INTIMACY. BUT JUST A LITTLE COMMON COMPANY.

64

Alone

I HAVE ALWAYS BEEN ALONE.

NO FRIENDS, SAVE FOR THE VARY FEW I RARELY SEE.

I HAVE A FAMILY, BUT THEY DON'T KNOW ME.

NO LOVE, NOT EVEN SIMPLE COMPANY.

I HAVE ALWAYS BEEN ALONE WITH ONLY MY MISERY.

65

Black Pencil

I WANT TO BE A BLACK WING, SOFT YET DARK.

BUT ALL I AM AS OD NOW IS A CHEAP BLACK PENCIL. RUGGED AND DULL WITH A BROKEN TIP.

66

Nine Billion Years

WE ONLY HAVE NINE BILLION YEARS, UNTIL WE ALL IN EVERY CONCEIVABLE WAY TURN TO DUST,

WHEN WE IN EVERY DEFINITION KNOWN TO US BEGIN TO FADE.

WHEN WE IN EVERY POSSIBLE MEANINGLESS MEANING RETURN TO COLD ENDLESS NIGHT AND THE ABSENCE OF LIGHT.

67

Is Charity Worth The Poverty

I HAVE FOUND MYSELF IN A PLACE I HAVE BEEN TRYING TO ESCAPE FROM.

I HAVE A DISEASE THAT KILLS ME SLOWLY, CHARITY.

68

Poem, I Forgot

A DAMN SHAME, I MAY HAVE LOST A POEM THAT WOULD HAVE LED ME TO FAME.

69

November

NOVEMBER, THE PERFECT MONTH BETWEEN OCTOBER AND DECEMBER.

HOLDING ALL WONDERS OF DECEMBER AND OCTOBER.

NOVEMBER BORES THE TREES OF OCTOBER. HOLDING BOLD COLORS OF OLD.

NOVEMBER BARES A DULL MONOCHROME SKY OF GRAY, NOTHING GAY.

NOVEMBER HAS THE WARM STILL OF THE SUMMER'S FALL. AND THE NORTH WIND CHILL OF THE DARK WINTER THRALL.

NOVEMBER IS THE HOST OF WHEN I STARTED TO DIE. THE SOURCE OF MANY INSPIRATIONS OF MINE.

70

It's Snowing

IT'S SNOWING. VARY, VARY SOFTLY...
IT'S SNOWING. VARY, VARY FAINTLY...
IT'S SNOWING. VARY, VARY LIGHTLY...

SO MUCH SO YOU CAN FEEL IT ON YOUR SKIN.
YOU CAN ONLY SEE IT IF YOU LOOK THROUGH THEW LIGHT OF A STREET LAMP.

71

Haunted

I AM HAUNTED BY THE CRIES OF A SMALL BOY.

I AM HAUNTED BY THE DREAMS OF A CHILDHOOD WITH NO JOY.

Melancholy In B7th

DROP D GUITAR TUNING
IN MELANCHOLIC SINGING
D AND A ALL IN MINOR AS WELL AS E
STRUM AWAY, PLAY FOR A LOVE LONGING
LET IT SING, SING ABOUT THE MIDNIGHT RAIN
SING ME A SONG ABOUT LOVE

73

The Rustling Of The Wind

IN THE ROARING THUNDER OF THE WIND BENDING THE TOWERS TO THEIR WILL, ALL I CAN HEAR IS MUSIC.

74

Fire In The Endless

I ONCE WROTE OF AN ENDLESS NIGHT. A VOID OF A PURPLE HUE OF SORTS. WITH FIRE ALL AROUND ME IN THE FORM OF LIGHTS. BIG AND SMALL, CLOSE AND FAR. SISTERS OF SEVEN PSYCHOPOMPS CRADLE ME THOUGH THAT ENDLESS EXPANSE OF FIRES THAT EMBRACED ME WITH WARMTH. AND I WAS KISSED BY THE COOL ENDLESS DARKNESS. I OFTEN FIND MYSELF IN THIS SPACE WHILE ASLEEP. OR EVEN IN THE BRIGHT LIGHT OF DAY. I WISH I COULD LIVE IN THIS DIMENSION FOREVER AND SLEEPED

75

He Who Made My School Days Bright

ALAS, MY MENTOR. I KNEW HIM ONLY FOR A FRACTION OF MY LIFE. AND YET I KNOWN NOT ANOTHER MAN OF SUCH QUALITY, FANCY. JEST AND CLOSE. THAT MAN HAFT TAUGHT ME TO WRITE. TAUGHT ME SONG IN LIFE. FIND AND GIVE MEANING TO MY OWN EXISTENCE, THAT MAN HAFT INSPIRED ME LIKE NO OTHER. HE WOULD DROWN THE ROOM IN LAUGHTER, BRING TALES AND STORIES TO LIFE. GIVING, GIFTING, GRANTING ME THE KNOWLEDGE I DESPERATELY DESIRED. EVEN THOUGH I AM NOT DESERVED. I NEVER DARED, DREAMED THAT I WOULD BE SO CLOSE TO THAT INFAMOUS IMMORTALITY. MY ONLY HOPE IS THAT HE TO BE REMEMBERED, LOVED FOR ETERNITY, FOR I SILL CHERISH HIM, EVEN AFTER I DIE.

76

A City Of Woodlands

LOOK AT THEM... THE COMMON MAN AND WOMAN. THE MUNDANE AND MUNDY. HOW MANY OF THEM DO YOU THINK ARE NOT WHAT THEY SEEM? WOLVES IN A SHEEP'S HERD. THEIR WORLD IS OF AN EVERGREEN FOREST OF MYSTERY. WHILE OURS IS A GRAY STAGE OF CONCRETE TREES AND GLASS. NO MAGIC, NO WONDER.

77

What I Do To The Art

I WAS ALWAYS WORKING HARD,
BUT IT WASN'T ALWAYS ART.
IT WAS JUST AN OLD PREMADE BOX,
THAT I SWIFTLY TORE APART.
I CUT AWAY THAT WAS PAINSTAKINGLY MADE,
AND GAVE IT A CHEAP BLACK COAT OF PAINT.
I RUINED SOMEONE'S WORK OF ART,
AND GAVE MY OWN LITTLE MARKS.

78

Way Back When

REMEMBER BACK THEM?

IN THE GOOD OLD DAYS... YES.

WAY BACK THEN WHEN GAS WAS A DOLLAR.

BACK IN THE DAY WHEN WE LIVED IN SQUALOR.

WHEN REBELS HAD MORE THAN JUST TEN SHOTS.

THE YEARS WHEN WE HAD AIDS IN LOTS.

79

Under A Scarlet Moon

I HAVE SAT HERE A THOUSAND TIMES.
WISHING, LONGING FOR BETTER DAYS.
DRINK IN HAND AND SMOKE IN THE AIR.
I NOTICED THEN THAT IN THE SKIES.
THE RAIN AND CLOUDS WERE PARTING WAYS.
THE MOON BRIGHTER THAN OUR OWN STAR.
SUDDENLY THE MOON WAS WANNING.
SOMETHING GREAT HAD SHADOWED THE MOON.
DIMMING, CLOUDING. TURNING IT DARK.
I STARED IN AWE, ALMOST CRYING.
AS THE MOON GLOWED A DARK MAROON.
I'VE NEVER SEEN SOMETHING SO STARK.
I SAW THIS BLOOD MOON AS A SIGN.

THAT I SHOULD SHED THE BLINDING LIGHT.

AND EMBRACE THE BEAUTIFUL NIGHT.

JOIN THE BATS AND RAVENS IN FLIGHT.

80

Moronics

I HAVE BEEN SO USED TO THE GLOOM OF OTHER PEOPLE'S MORONICS. THAT I HAVE BECOME DEATH TO AND DUMB TO MY OWN HARMONICS.

81

My People

TO YOU MY BEAUTIFUL GOTHIC PEOPLE...

TO YOU MY GOTHIC KING IN THE STEEL STEEPLE...

TO YOU, THE OUTCASTS, THE NON-CONFORMISTS, THE REBEL.

I JUST WANT TO SAY, I LOVE YOU, I ADORE YOU, I THANK YOU.

82

Melancholic Misery

I FEEL I AM IN A PERPETUAL STATE OF
MELANCHOLY AND MISERY.

83

The Way They Talk

I HAVE NOTICED THAT IN ALL MY YOUTH AND MOST OF MY YOUNGER DAYS.

PEOPLE, PARTNERS, PROFESSIONALS. TALKED AT ME IN ALL SORTS OF UNFORTUNATE WAYS.

THEY SPOKE TO ME AS IF MY MIND WAS AT A DELAY.

THEY TALKED AT ME AS IF INTENTIONALLY MY MANNERS WERE AWAY, OR SO THEY SAY...

DO THEY TALK TO ME LIKE A SOUND MINDED HUMAN? NAY...

WILL THEY SPEAK TO ME AS IF I AM AN IDIOT? IMBECILIC? AND NOT A POET? ALWAYS...

84

Where Do I Belong?

WHERE DO I GO?
HOW DO I GET OUT?
WHAT CAN I DO?
WHY CAN'T I NOT DOUBT?
WHERE IS MY HOME?
WHO IS MY ROUTE?
TO KNOW WHERE I BELONG...

85

What Is The Darkness?

FEW PEOPLE ASK ME... MORE SO NO ONE ASKS ME.

WHAT IS THIS DARKNESS? BLACKNESS? BLEAKNESS?

THAT I LOVE AND CHERISH SO MUCH.

TO BE HONEST. I CAN'T REALLY EXPLAIN IN A WAY THAT MAKES SENSE TO MOST.

ALL THAT I CAN REALLY SAY IS THAT...

THE DARKNESS IS REAL. THE MOST HONEST, BEAUTIFUL, REAL THING IN MY LIFE AND I LOVE IT.

EVEN MORE THAN I LOVE MYSELF.

86

Deadwood

WHOMEVER THOUGHT I WOULD SHARE IDENTITY WITH A TREE? A SOLITARY DEADWOOD TREE BARE AND QUITE GRAY. SURROUNDED BY LUSCIOUS GREEN LEAVES.

HOW LONELY THIS TREE... MUST BE. LIKE ME. DIFFERENT FROM HER NEIGHBORS, LIKE ME, DARKER THAN THE OTHERS.

87

A Windy Day

ON A DAY LIKE THIS CIGAR IN BRUISED HAND.

THE WIND CARRYING SMOKE IN THE DISTANCE.

I WISH I COULD RIDE THAT WAVE OF WIND LIKE FOAM IN THE SAND.

TAKE ME AWAY TO A BETTER PLACE.

88

It Is Raining

IT IS RAINING, WITH A SINGLE GRAIN OF SUNSHINE. MOST TRY TO CATCH THE RAYS. BUT I JUST DRINK THE RAIN.

89

My Friend The Moon

ALWAYS THERE TO SAY HELLO.

SMILING DOWN WITH A SHINING YELLOW.

EVEN IF THE GLOW ISN'T SO STARK.

I CAN STILL SEE MY FRIENDS SHADOW IN THE DARK.

90

At The Faire

SITING AT A BENCH AN ELF JUST WALKED PAST ME.

SIPPING HOMEMADE WINE, BEAUTIFUL CREATURES IS ALL I SEE.

HANGING IN THE RAFTERS, LANTERNS BURNING BRIGHT.

RESTING ON THE GROUND FLOWERS ALL AROUND.

ROLLING IN THE TREES, THE MISTY FOG SINGS.

WE ALL ARE LAUGHING DOWN THE HALLWAYS, SMILING ALWAYS.

91

Cry You Mortals

BY GOD, BY DEITY, BY DEATH...
FOREVER SHALL I CRY.
BUT WHY? AM I THE ONLY ONE WHO CRIES?
FACES ALL OVER, AND NOT A SINGLE ONE SOMBER.
DYING PEOPLE, SUFFERING, HEARTBREAKING...
AND I AM HE ONLY ONE WHO SHEDS A TEAR.
TO CARE FOR OTHERS SUFFERING AND FEAR.
IS THIS WHAT IT MEANS TO BE HUMAN, OR IS THIS MY LACK OF HUMANITY?

92

The Queen Of Instruments

KEYS LIKE A PIANO.

PIPES LIKE A GIANT FLUTE.

A GOD'S BREATH TO AWAKEN A NOTE IN THE THOUSANDS.

A KEY CAN SHAKE A BUILDING.

A NOTE CAN SHATTER BONE.

THROUGH MILES IT CAN BE FELT.

FOR DAYS ITS RESONANCE CAN BE FELT.

LIKE A MEMORY.

93

The Beauty and Tragedy Of A Stogie

SWEET SAVORY SMOKE
FINE, FANTASTIC FIRE
PERFECT PEACEFUL PLEASURE
RESTFUL RELAXATION RISING
MUSE MUSING MELODIES
LONGING LONELINESS LOST
THEN THE EMBERS FADE.

94

For You, For Me, For It

THIS IS FOR THE TEARS THAT'S YET TO SHED.

THIS IS FOR THE ONES WHO AREN'T YET DEAD.

THIS IS FOR THE ENDLESS SENSE OF DREAD,

THIS IS FOR THE COLD THAT NEVER ENDS.

THIS IS FOR THE WORDS THAT CAN'T BE UNSAID.

THIS IS FOR THE PAIN OF THE INSANE WHO SING.

THIS IS FOR THE BROKEN TRAIN TO FAME,

THIS IS FOR THE UNKNOWN NAMES, AND THE MONEY NEVER GAINED.

95

Snap Twice

I SHARE SOMETHING WITH A FAMOUS FAMILY, A LAST NAME, PARTLY.

ONLY THING MISSING IS A SINGLE LETTER. ASIDE FROM THAT. I FEEL I AM A LOST CHILD FROM THIS FAMILY.

I'M CREEPY AND I'M COOKY, MYSTERIOUS AND SPOOKY, A LITTLE BIT OOKY. BUT ALL TOGETHER I AM LONELY.

96

To My Brother, To My Friend, To My Fellow Poet.

AS TRADITION I WRITE A LETTER AT THE END OF MY POETIC WORKS. TO SOMEONE OR SOMETHING. WHETHER IT BE A TANGIBLE REAL CONCEPT OF PHYSICAL SUBSTANCE. OR SOME ELDRITCH CONCEPTS SEEDED FROM THE RECESSES OF THE MELANCHOLIC MIND. I WISH TO TRANSCRIBE THESE THOUGHTS INTO POETRY OR STORIES, BUT I FEEL WHAT SOME ONLY SEE IS RAMBLINGS AND SCRIBBLINGS OF AN IMBECILIC MADMAN. MY CONGREGATION AS I LIKE TO SAY IS GROWING AT THE SPEED OF A BIRD WITH A BROKEN WING. BUT STILL, I HAVE HOPELESS HOPE TO GROW MY CHURCH, AND BE A LORD AMONGST THE CONFORMIST POPULOUS. I HAVE YOU TO THANK FOR MY WORK AND SENSE OF SELF-WORTH. THANK YOU, WILLIAM.

SINCERELY, R. BLACK

www.ingramcontent.com/pod-product-compliance
Lightning Source LLC
LaVergne TN
LVHW051953060526
838201LV00059B/3625